D0491302

Cuddle!

Written by
Beth Shoshan

Illustrated by
Jacqueline East

little bee

First published in 2006 by Meadowside Children's Books, 185 Fleet Street, London, EC4A 2HS
This edition published in 2007 by Little Bee, an imprint of Meadowside Children's Books

Illustrations © Jacqueline East 2006
The right of Jacqueline East to be identified as the illustrator of this work has been asserted by her in accordance with the Copyright, Designs and Patents Act, 1988
A CIP catalogue record for this book is available from the British Library
Printed in Indonesia

10 9 8 7 6 5 4 3 2

I'd cuddle a whale,
but I might be
too small,

I'd cuddle
a giraffe,
but I think
he's too tall.

I'd cuddle
a hedgehog
but, ouch!,
they're so spiky,

I'd cuddle a crocodile.

If I cuddled
a gorilla

I would end up
much thinner,

If I cuddled a tiger
I'd end up as dinner.

I'd cuddle a skunk
but I think they're
too smelly,

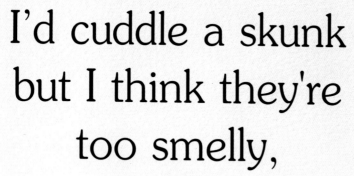

I'd cuddle a shark

but I'd be in his belly!

I'd cuddle
a python

way up high
in a tree

I'd cuddle
a hippo
who might just
squash me.

I'd cuddle a lion

but he'd bite off my head,

Do you think I can cuddle my Teddy instead?